Praises for
The Beauty of my Skin

The beauty of this book is in the great truths of its simple text and the warmth and sensitivity of its illustrations. It is a celebration of beauty-both of the shades and hues of black skin and the intimate relationships between loving adults and loving children.

— Dr. Steve Seidel,
Director of Arts in Education
Harvard Graduate School of Education

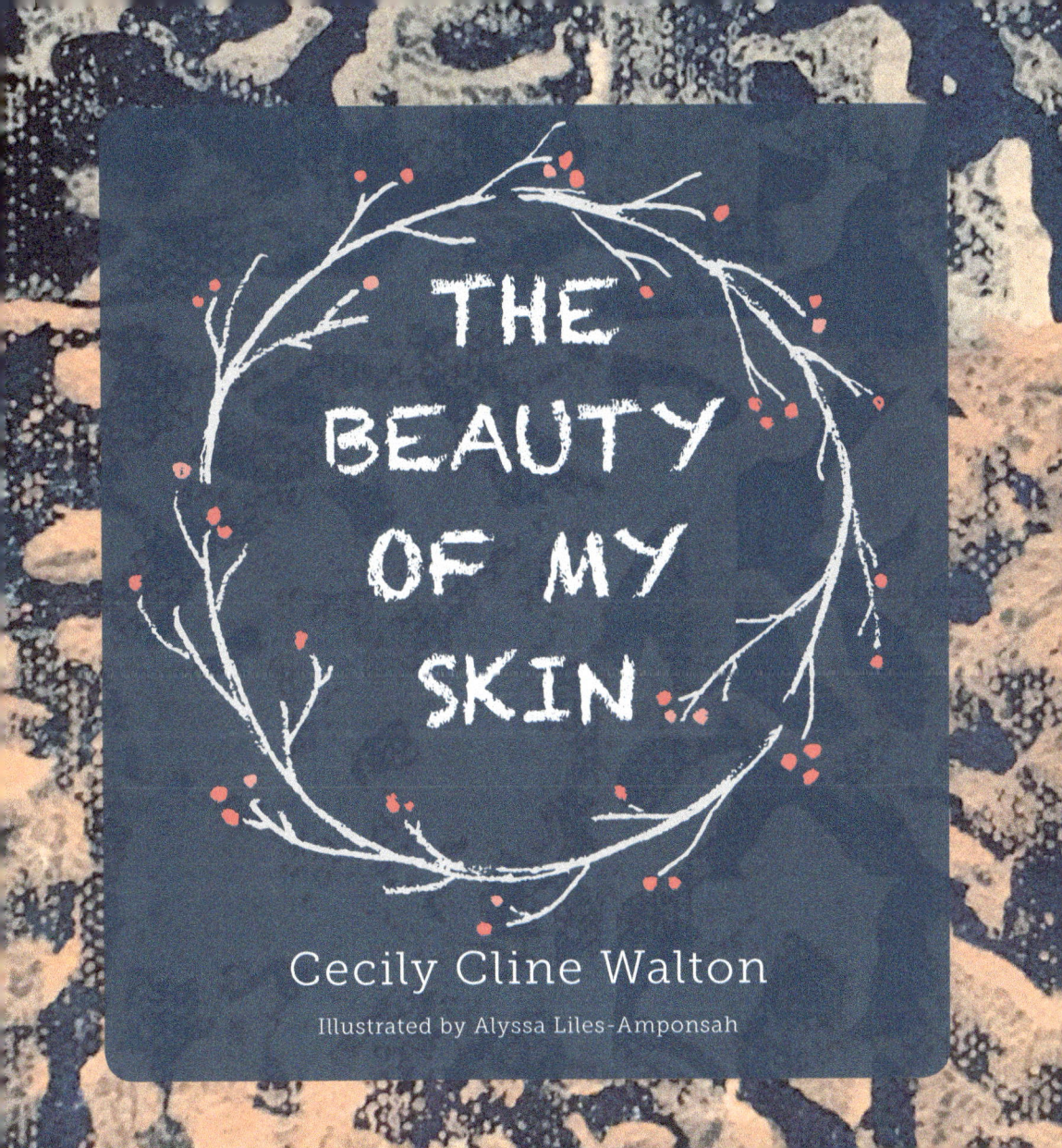

WWW.13THANDJOAN.COM

The Beauty of My Skin. Copyright © 2018 by Cecily Cline Walton. All rights reserved. No part of this publication may be reproduced, distributed, or transmitted in any form or by any means, including photocopying, recording, or other electronic or mechanical methods, without the prior written permission of the publisher, except in the case of brief quotations embodied in critical reviews and certain other noncommercial uses permitted by copyright law. For permission requests, write to the publisher, addressed "Attention: Permissions Coordinator," 500 N. Michigan Avenue, Suite #600, Chicago, IL 60611.

13th & Joan books may be purchased for educational, business or sales promotional use. For information, please email the Sales Department at sales@13thandjoan.com.

Printed in the U.S.A.
First Printing, June 2018
Library of Congress Cataloging-in-Publication Data
has been applied for.
ISBN 978-1-7324712-6-9

All images are copyrighted to Alyssa Liles-Amponsah

DEDICATION

To my amazing three children:,
Zora Neale, Elijah Mays and Baldwin Cline
Thank you for making me a better person

Love you the Most,
MOMMY

For all the wonderful families and children that allowed me to share in their lives, Thank you!!

In Beauty,
CECILY

For Aalia and August and all of the beautiful children in my life. Thank you for inspiring me!

Love,
ALYSSA

There is no one like me anywhere.

The beauty of my skin

There is no one like me anywhere.

The beauty of my skin

Sweet butterscotch kisses

There is no one like me anywhere.

The beauty of my skin.

The beauty of my skin.

Thank you for giving me the beautiful skin that I am in.

About
The Author

Cecily Cline Walton is an avid lover of all books. She is a proud mother of three and resides between Cambridge, MA, and Atlanta, GA.

About

The Illustrator

Alyssa Liles-Amponsah is an Artist and Educator. She is the mother of two and is currently based in Philadelphia, PA. See more of Alyssa's work at:

WWW.ALYSSALILESAMPONSAH.COM

www.ingramcontent.com/pod-product-compliance
Lightning Source LLC
Chambersburg PA
CBHW061146070526
44584CB00033B/4433